100

HEALING SCRIPTURES

&

PRAYERS

FOR

SELF-DELIVERANCE

Activating God's Creative power and divine medicine through the Spoken Words, Faith and Affirmation

JOHN IJEH

All rights reserved Copyright © 2020 John Ijeh

No part of this book may be reproduced in any form without permission in writing from the publisher except in the case of brief quotation for church related publication, critical articles or reviews

All scripture quotations are from the King James Version, unless otherwise stated

+2348060248601

Email ijehjohn@rocketmail.com

OTHER BOOKS BY JOHN IJEH

- Demon possession and satanic altars
- How to overcome witchcraft and demonic attacks
- Deliverance from stagnation and evil family pattern
- Stand up and Fight
- Command your Finances
- How to receive healing and deliverance from God's word
- Teach your child to pray
- How to Identify and overcome Suicide Spirit
- How to Receive Healing and Deliverance through God's word
- Miracle Prayers for Divine Healing and Deliverance
- Towards a Blissful Marriage
- 120 Spiritual Warfare prayers to Crush Witchcraft and demonic Attacks
- 101 Dangerous Midnight Prayers to Break Stubborn Obstacles and Satanic Strongholds

CONTENTS

INTRODUCTION 5

Chapter One 7

Bible Facts about Healing................................7

Sickness did not originate from God. 7

Sin Brought about Sickness. 8

Satan is the Architect of Sickness and Disease 9

Simple Act of Faith Brings Result 11

Chapter Two 13

The Power of Faith 13

Our Unbelief Hurts God 15

It's up to you..16

If you can Believe: you will Obtain 17

Your Faith Excites Him 19

Chapter Three 22

Examples of Healing in the Bible.................22

Abraham and Abimelech 22

Naaman the Leper 23

The Leper in Mathew 24

The Woman with the Issue of Blood 25

The Paralytic 28

The Cripple at the Beautiful Gate 32

Chapter Four 35

Hindrances to Healing 35

Why Is Everyone Not Healed? 39

What's the deal with that? 41

Hindrance #1 – Un-Forgiveness 42

Hindrance #2 Un-Confessed Sin 47

Hindrance #3 – Healing Process 49

#4 God is Using My Sickness to Teach Me a Lesson 53

Hindrance #4 – Lack of Persistence 54

Hindrance #5 – Unbelief 60

Ignorance of the Character of God! 66

Chapter Five 69

Healing Scriptures 69

Chapter Six 84

PRAYING WITH THE SCRIPTURES 84

1# Hear the Word 86

3#Speak the Word 89

Act on the Word 92

The Woman with the Issue of Blood 94

First of all, she heard about Jesus. 97

She said to herself 100

She Acted 102

A Unique Model 104

Faith Proclamation 1 107

Faith Proclamation 2 109

Faith proclamation 3 110

Chapter Seven 112

Seven Days Prayer Journal for Healing and Deliverance 112

Day One 113

Day Two 115

Day Three 118

Day Four 121

Day Five 124

Day Six 127

Day Seven 131

ABOUT THE AUTHOR 135

INTRODUCTION

The world today is ravaged by a strange disease. Almost everyone and every nation under heaven is under siege. People are confused as to what the way out is for humanity. No time in human history has there been such fear and concern at a global scale. Science and technology seem to be very feeble in the face of this common enemy. The question is whether there is a way out for humanity and the answer is yes. The word of God holds the solution to every human problem. God has provided healing and cur for us in His word. His word holds the solution. The Bible says that God sent is word and healed them and delivered them from their destruction.

When we reach out to God in faith, our healing and deliverance are sure. It shall come to pass that whosoever shall call on the name of the lord shall be delivered. There is salvation, healing and deliverance to anyone who comes to God by faith.

Throughout the history of God's dealing with men, he has always demonstrated his readiness to help man out of his predicaments. God wants you well. He wants you healed and in sound health. Sickness is not a gift from him; it is a gift from Satan. God demonstrated his healing power both in the Old Testament and in the church age.

Chapter One

Bible Facts about Healing

Many people are not aware that God is more interested in their wellbeing than they are themselves. In other words, God cares about you more than you care about yourself. he wants you healed more than you wants yourself out of that bed of affliction. I want to show you some Bible facts about healing.

Sickness did not originate from God.

It is quite hard for people to believe this statement. Their argument is that it is God who created all things including sickness. Well, sickness was never part of God's creation. The account of creation in Genesis 1 and 2 didn't mention sickness as one of those things that God created. When God created the heaven and earth, he saw that everything he made was good. Everything God made was good but you and I know that sickness is not a good thing. No one is ever happy being sick. Nobody has ever come to testify to the goodness of God for making him or her sick

Sin Brought about Sickness.

Sickness was introduced when man disobeyed his maker at the Garden of Eden. Before Adam and Eve ate the forbidden fruit, they never knew anything like pain, sickness or sorrow. All these came into our world as a result of sin. Sin has promoted pain and sorrow in our world.

Sin caused separation between God and man. The devil took advantage of that separation to afflict man with all kinds of sickness and disease.

Satan is the Architect of Sickness and Disease

Man was deceived by the devil. The devil is the one who brought calamity upon humanity.

How art thou fallen from heaven, O Lucifer, son of the morning! how art thou cut down to the ground, which didst weaken the nations! Isaiah 14:12

This scripture confirms that it was the fall of Satan that brought about calamity to the human race. He is the one who introduced sin to the world. The Bible calls him the man of sin.

Jesus came purposely to destroy the works of the devil. Understand that the primary reason of Jesus coming to the world was to undo what Satan has done. The devil deceived man and consequently put him in bondage. Jesus came to destroy the works of the devil and free man from his bondage. The Bible in John 10: ten tells us that the devil came to steal, kill and destroy but Jesus came to us life in abundance.

Whenever the devil visits, he leaves a trail of lost, death and destruction behind. Those are his hallmarks and signature. Lost, death and destruction only signal the presence of Satan. Jesus gives life wherever He appears. He came to give us life in its fullness. 1John 4 tells us that Jesus came to destroy the works of Satan. This includes, sickness, disease, death, lost and destruction.

All through Jesus' ministry, we see Him heal the sick and deliver those who were oppressed by demonic powers. He was passionate about giving people sound health and delivering them from oppression. At some points, he got so hard on religious folks for being more concerned about keeping the Sabbath law than setting those who were under the bondage of the devil free. He rebuke the chief priest who and the religious leaders who were cynical about his healing of the woman with infirmity for eighteen years and the man with the withered hand.

Simple Act of Faith Brings Result

Healing comes from God but majorly as a response to our faith. The Bible says that the prayer of faith will heal the sick

Is any sick among you? let him call for the elders of the church; and let them pray over him, anointing him with oil in the name of the Lord: And the prayer of faith shall save the sick, and the Lord shall raise him up; and if he have committed sins, they shall be forgiven him. James 5:14-15

The major point I want you to see in the scriptures above is the fact that faith is a vital element in the healing of sickness. James tells us with assurance that the prayer of faith will heal the sick. When we pray or act in faith, the result will be certain and undeniable. Many people don't get healed because they don't understand this. The healing power of God is attracted by our faith not our cry or pain. Your pain and cry don't move God, your faith does.

Chapter Two

The Power of Faith

Throughout the history of God's dealing with man, He has always long for men and women who will trust Him. The greatest need of God is in His relationship with man is not worship. There're numerous angels and heavenly beings who worship Him day and night. The Bible talks about the four living creatures and the twenty-four elders who worship Him day and night. Man is too sinful to stand before the presence a holy God. So, being allowed into His presence is an extravagant act of divine mercy.

The greatest need of God is trust. He wants men and women to trust Him. He is always searching for individuals who will repose their trust absolutely in Him. God gets so excited whenever he sees someone who has faith in him. His greatest need is to be trusted. He wants you to take Him by His words. His dealing with man is based on trust. The only to get him to act on your behalf is to trust Him.

Trust is so important to God that He considers it an act of righteousness. The Bible tells us that Abraham believed God and it was accounted to him as righteousness. Your trust in Him qualifies you before God.

Jesus tells us that the work of God is to believe in the one He has sent. The people were asking Him for what to do in order to do the work of God but Jesus told them that the work of God is not in doing but in trusting. You do the work of God by accepting what He has done through His son Jesus Christ. If you don't believe in the finished work of Christ, you are just playing religion.

Our Unbelief Hurts God

God is hurt when we doubt Him and He gets excited when we exercise our faith in His word. To doubt Him is to limit His power in our lives. God is looking for those who will not limit Him through doubt and unbelief. He wants to have a free flow in our lives; He doesn't want to be hindered. All things are possible to those who refuse to limit God in their lives.

The angel Gabriel was angry with Zachariah for doubting his message. In fact, he punished Zachariah for his unbelief. He said to Zachariah "I am Gabriel who stands in the presence of God; how dare you doubt a message I bring to you from the all powerful God'.

God considers doubting him as an insult. We belittle him with our unbelief and He doesn't like to be belittled. What God will do in your life is only limited by you and not anyone else or any force.

When Jesus got to Nazareth, his home town, the Bible tells us that his people doubted him. Because of their unbelief, Jesus couldn't do much miracles there except that he laid hands on few folks and healed them.

If they hadn't doubted Him, He would have done as much miracles in Nazareth as He did in other places.

It's up to you

Faith is so important in deciding whether or not we receive the miracle or answer we longed for. We see this in the ministry of

Jesus. When people come to him for healing or miracle, He let them know of the place of their faith in getting the answer they seek. He told them it was up to them to receive or not.

It's up to you to receive your healing or not. Healing is available. Jesus has paid for our wellbeing and deliverance on the cross. He is not going to pay another price. He paid it once and for all and he paid it in full. The whole salvation benefits are ours for the taking. Heaven is not going to hinder anyone from appropriating any of the salvation packages made available for us.

God has no limitation whatsoever, the challenge is with those who come to him for miracle and the problem was lack of faith

If you can Believe: you will Obtain

A man whose son was tormented by an evil spirit carried passionately to Jesus for help.

He narrated he brought the child to the disciples of Jesus but they couldn't do anything. He asked the master to take pity on him, or at least the little child. Jesus told him that pity doesn't command result in the kingdom, faith does. He told the man that it was up to him if his son would be delivered or not. If you can believe, all things are possible. In other words: it your faith that will set the boy free.

In another scenario, Jesus asked two blind men who came to Him for healing: Do you believe I am able to do this?

Why would He ask such question? Was he looking for affirmation from the blind men or did he need the faith of the men to strengthen His own faith? The answer is no. he didn't need any of that. He wanted to make sure the men were in a position to receive.

The things of God are things of faith. Without faith you can't receive. Your faith is the assurance you have for the things you seek. It is the proof of eligibility. You are eligible because you believe. You are qualified because you trust Him. Those who trust the Lord are qualified for healing, miracle or whatever they seek.

Your Faith Excites Him

I have established earlier that the greatest need of God in His relationship with men is faith. He derives pleasure from our absolute trust and dependent on Him. Your faith makes Him leap for joy. To exercise faith in Him is to pleasure His heart. When you use your faith, you make God happy. Your faith takes limitation off God.

God has always struggled with men and women who limit Him. He invests so much energy in getting people to trust Him totally.

So, whenever He sees someone who demonstrates faith in Him, he gets excited.

Healing evangelists have faced one particular challenge in their ministry and that is getting people to believe God wants them healed. Many would rather believe that the sickness they have is for a purpose or God is using it to teach them a lesson.

Well, maybe your sickness has a purpose. That's right! Everything in life has a purpose. The purpose of that sickness in your body right now is to get healed. It is there for you to send it off and enjoy a good health.

Jesus told His disciples in John 9, that the man was born blind was for the power of to be made manifest.

Jesus always commended those who demonstrate faith. The woman with the issue of blood was told that it was her faith that made her whole. The Syrophonician woman was commended for her great faith. The centurion was admired by Jesus for his faith. All these individuals got the answer they sought. Faith never fails.

Jesus was harder on His disciples for not believing than he was on the woman caught in the act of adultery or the Samaritan woman who had married five husbands and living with a sixth who was not even a husband. This goes to demonstrate the importance of faith in dealing with God. God doesn't condone sin of any kind but He considers unbelief the worst sin any man can commit.

Chapter Three

Examples of Healing in the Bible

There're several instances of healing in the Bible. We shall consider a few of them.

Abraham and Abimelech

Abimelech had taken Sarah the wife of Abraham because he lied that she was his sister. God came to Abimelech in a dream and threaten to kill him if he refuses to restore Sarah to Abraham. By now Abimelech's household had been plagued by strange sickness. When he obeyed and restored Abraham his wife, Abraham prayed and God healed the entire household of Abimelech.

This is one of the first cases of divine healing in the Bible. The healing here was an answer to simple prayer of faith. We were not even told that Abraham fasted or performed any rituals

Naaman the Leper

The story of Prophet Elisha and Naaman the Syrian is a popular one. Naaman was leprous. He came to Elisha for healing. The man of God told him to go deep himself in Jordan River seven times. At first Naaman felt insulted. His reason was that there were better rivers in Syria than Israel. If bathing in the river was all it takes to be healed, he would rather do in his home country in a cleaner river. One of his servants persuaded him to obey and when he did he was cleansed of his leprosy.

Here we see again a simple act of faith. Though Naaman didn't believe at first, when he obeyed, he got the result he wanted. The healing power of God is attracted by a simple act of faith. The prayer doesn't need to be long neither does it requires any rituals- just believe and you will receive.

The Leper in Mathew

A leper came to Jesus and asked if Jesus was willing to heal him. If you are willing, you can make me whole.

This is exactly the approach of so many individuals when it comes to healing. They are not sure what the will of the Lord is. Some know that God is able to heal but they are not sure he is willing to heal them. Jesus answered that question in his response to the leper. "I will, be thou healed."

Here Jesus settled the question of whether God wants to heal or not. He wants to heal you. Let that settle in your heart. He has no pleasure in your pain. He is delighted to see you healthy. It doesn't matter what type of disease it is; God doesn't need to go for more training to acquire extra power in other to heal you. Corona virus disease is not superior to headache before God.

The Woman with the Issue of Blood

Lk. 8:43 And a woman having an issue of blood twelve years, which had spent all her living upon physicians, neither could be healed of any,

44 Came behind him, and touched the border of his garment: and immediately her issue of blood stanched.

45 And Jesus said, Who touched me? When all denied, Peter and they that were with him said, Master, the multitude throng thee and press thee, and sayest thou, Who touched me?

46 And Jesus said, Somebody hath touched me: for I perceive that virtue is gone out of me.

47 And when the woman saw that she was not hid, she came trembling, and falling down before him, she declared unto him before all the people for what cause she had touched him, and how she was healed immediately.

48 And he said unto her, Daughter, be of good comfort: thy faith hath made thee whole; go in peace.

The story of this woman clearly shows the efficacy of radical faith. Here we see that you can take your healing by force. The woman didn't wait for Jesus to pray for her. She had suffer so much for such wait, she just stretched her hand and took her healing while others were busy thronging Jesus.

God admires such faith. I told you earlier that God gets excited when we exercise our faith. Faith is such a strong force that can't go unrecognized. The moment the woman touched Jesus, He felt something left him. He stopped and asked "Who touched me?" His disciple couldn't understand why Jesus should ask such question in the face of a huge crowd all trying to touch Him.

Peter quickly told him that such question was unnecessary. Master, a lot of people are touching you; you can't single out a particular person in this marmot crowd.

No, Jesus replied, I felt a different touch from the usual touch of the crowd. I perceive that virtue has gone out of me.

The woman came out trembling and confessed to her action. Jesus told her that her faith had made her whole.

The reason Jesus wanted the woman to own up was to let the crowd know that they could receive answers to their problems by faith.

You can lay hold of the promises of God and receive your healing. It's okay to have someone pray for you, but you can do it yourself; just hold on to God's word and continue to confess it over your situation.

The Paralytic

Luke 5:17 And it came to pass on a certain day, as he was teaching, that there were Pharisees and doctors of the law sitting by, which were come out of every town of Galilee, and Judaea, and Jerusalem: and the power of the Lord was present to heal them.

18 And, behold, men brought in a bed a man which was taken with a palsy: and they sought means to bring him in, and to lay him before him.

19 And when they could not find by what way they might bring him in because of the multitude, they went upon the housetop, and let him down through the tiling with his couch into the midst before Jesus.

20 And when he saw their faith, he said unto him, Man, thy sins are forgiven thee.

21 And the scribes and the Pharisees began to reason, saying, Who is this which speaketh blasphemies? Who can forgive sins, but God alone?

22 But when Jesus perceived their thoughts, he answering said unto them, What reason ye in your hearts?

23 Whether is easier, to say, Thy sins be forgiven thee; or to say, Rise up and walk?

24 But that ye may know that the Son of man hath power upon earth to forgive sins, (he said unto the sick of the palsy,) I say unto thee, Arise, and take up thy couch, and go into thine house.

25 And immediately he rose up before them, and took up that whereon he lay, and departed to his own house, glorifying God.

26 And they were all amazed, and they glorified God, and were filled with fear, saying, We have seen strange things to day.

This is another story of healing in the Bible. This man had been paralyzed for a better part of his life. That day his friends decided to do something remarkable for him. They heard that Jesus was in a house healing everyone that was sick. They brought him to the place but unfortunately, the whole place was overcrowded. They could only stay in the overflow. Well, these young men decided to take off the roof of the house where Jesus was and lowered the man in front of Jesus. That singular act of faith impressed Jesus and the man went home healed.

Here again we see the place of faith in receiving our healing. Faith is a force that will always attract God's attention whenever it is demonstrated. I have mentioned earlier that God gets excited when we demonstrate faith in His word. Such excitement won't let Him turn away from you. Anyone who approaches God by faith must have an answer.

Hebrew 11:6 tells us that without faith, it is impossible to please God. Your cry or pain does not move Him your faith does. If you're in pain and refuses to believe or put your trust in Him, God assumes you don't need his help. He will go to the one who is comfortable but has faith in His word. He will give such individual more comfort and bless that person the more. You have to believe if you want to receive.

God is attracted to those who want to please Him. The Bible says that the eye of the Lord moves to and fro upon the earth to show Himself strong on behalf of those whose hearts are perfect towards Him.

When Jesus saw the faith of these young men, He couldn't help but grant their heart desire.

No act of faith is overlooked by God. God respects our faith. He can't ignore a prayer of faith. James tells us that the prayer of will heal the sick.

The Cripple at the Beautiful Gate

The crippled man at the beautiful gate is another example of healing in the Bible. The story demonstrates the fact that the disciples of Jesus understood that they too could heal the sick and deliver those who were oppressed just like their master

Ac 3:1 Now Peter and John went up together into the temple at the hour of prayer, being the ninth hour.

2 And a certain man lame from his mother's womb was carried, whom they laid daily at the gate of the temple which is called Beautiful, to ask alms of them that entered into the temple;

3 Who seeing Peter and John about to go into the temple asked an alms.

4 And Peter, fastening his eyes upon him with John, said, Look on us.

5 And he gave heed unto them, expecting to receive something of them.

6 Then Peter said, Silver and gold have I none; but such as I have give I thee: In the name of Jesus Christ of Nazareth rise up and walk.

7 And he took him by the right hand, and lifted him up: and immediately his feet and ankle bones received strength.

8 And he leaping up stood, and walked, and entered with them into the temple, walking, and leaping, and praising God.

The disciples of Jesus had just been baptized in the Holy Ghost and a new movement had just started. The Pharisees and other religious leaders were grappling with how to quench this new movement when this notable miracle happened.

Peter and John were going to the temple to pray. At the gate of the temple was a beggar whose health condition had condemned to begging for a living. When he saw Peter and John, he thought of business as usual. He asked them for alms but instead of receiving alms, he got the shock of his life; he was healed never to be a cripple again

Chapter Four

Hindrances to Healing

The world has made a very astonishing advancement in the field of medical science. We now have the equipment to diagnose and cure different types of sicknesses. But despite all the medications we use today there are still a lot of people everywhere around us who are suffering from all kinds of sicknesses, pain and injuries. It seems as if diseases increase and multiply with every advance we make in the field of medicine.

Despite our modern technology and all the great progresses we seem to have made in the medical fields we are still in need of a lot of healing-humanity is still writhing in pains and infirmities.

There's more need of doctors and health workers today than ever before. Back in the day of Jesus' ministry on earth, there would have been very few doctors and medications. The Apostles recorded such tremendous healing miracles that even the shadow of Peter and apron taken from the body of Paul were healing the sick.

Paul was shipwrecked on the island of Malta; the result was that he got all the sick folks on that island healed. This is simply because Paul understood the place of healing in the redemptive package. The situation he was in didn't rob him of God's ability to work through him.

He was on that island as a common criminal. He appealed to Cesar when he saw the game the Jewish men were trying to play with Governor Felix. On his way to Rome, he was shipwrecked and finally landed on this unusual island. The narrator tells us that the people of the island of Malta were barbaric. (which means they were cruel and uncivilized) yet Paul demonstrated the power of God to heal the sick among them.

Most people today who got sick would rather grin and bear it as part of what is involved in being humans. Divine healing is looked upon as such a big mystery. People can't understand why God should take any delight in getting sick folks healed. But Jesus demonstrated God's concern for our physical wellbeing when He came along and started freely healing people from all kinds of sicknesses and diseases. His action clearly shows what the will of God is concerning our physical wellbeing. He never refused anyone who approached Him for healing or deliverance

Jesus was not the only one who demonstrated this great concern of our loving father; He gave the same power and authority to His disciple and they too went about destroying sickness and disease in people's lives

(Luke 9:1-2 (NLT) 1 One day Jesus called together his twelve disciples and gave them power and authority to cast out demons and to heal all diseases. 2 Then he sent them out to tell everyone about the Kingdom of God and to heal the sick.
If today you are a disciple of Jesus Christ then you also has been given the same power to do what Jesus and the early apostle did. You can heal the sick and free those who are in pain.

Jesus even said that we will be able to do greater things than He did.

Today, there are more believers in Christ Jesus than in any previous age. If every Christian stand in the authority of Christ and demonstrate the power that is available to all of us, we would rid the world of the burden of sickness and disease.

The disciple never doubted the ability of God upon them; they went out and did exactly what Jesus said they would. Wherever they went, they left their mark of healing and deliverance. They went out from village to village and city to city preaching the gospel and healing the sick.

Why Is Everyone Not Healed?

It battles me that in a meeting where the power of God is awesome, some get healed while others don't. Is it that God is selective in administering His healing power? Are there individuals who are destined to be healed while others will bear their pain no matter how much they pray or demonstrate their faith for healing?

If we say that God is just then we must have to look elsewhere to find where the problem is. It is obvious that the problem is not with God or His ability to heal; it's with the man or the woman in need of healing.

Most people come for healing with a lot of preconceived notions. They stand in the line to be prayed for yet their idea about divine healing doesn't run concurrently with the scriptures. These notions are the things that stop them from receiving from God.

The Spirit of God is super sensitive. He works in line with divine purpose. He conforms only to the standard of God's word and nothing more. So, whatever contradicts God's word doesn't get His attention. This is why you can pray for two people with the same ailment at the same time; one will get healed and the other will not.

What's the deal with that?

There are some potential hindrances to healing. We shall look at few of them. This is by no means an exhaustive list but it is some of the major hindrances I have seen.

It has been my experience that most unbelievers get healed even when they may have never heard from God or ever read the bible. They may have no faith or not even believe in healing and they certainly are most likely to have unresolved sin issues in their life, yet they get healed most of the time.

Many of the people Jesus prayed for would have fallen into this category even if they were Jews and yet they too were healed. So what are the hindrances that can stop some Christian people receiving their healing?

Hindrance #1 – Un-Forgiveness

A lot of people live with grudge and bitterness in their hearts. They have unresolved anger and un-forgiveness in their hearts. People who carry resentment from un-forgiveness rarely receive healing or miracles.

The Bible says that if you do not from your heart forgive those who offend you neither will your heavenly father forgive your own sins.

The only reason you are qualified to receive healing miracle is because Jesus has paid for it. He has purchased our freedom from sin, sickness and spiritual death. Base on the finished work of Christ, our sins have been forgiven. But we are instructed to forgive those who have offended us as God for Christ sake has forgiven us. To go against this divine injunction is to forfeit our right to our salvation benefits.

There is a story of a woman who was very sick. Her entire body was full of boils. She had taken all kinds of medication and nothing was working. Finally, she turned to God for healing. She kept coming to this meeting for healing but wasn't healed. Others were receiving their healing except this woman. The man of God was worried and was asking God why the woman couldn't get healed. Then God revealed to him to ask the woman about her sister.

The man of God obeyed and asked the woman to tell him about her sister. Immediately, this woman's countenance changed. She became livid with anger-you could feel the vibration of the anger in her.

I don't want to talk about my sister man of God. If that will make God not to heal me so be it but I will never forgive my sister.

It took the man of God time to show this woman from the scripture that she must forgive her sister if she wants God to heal her.

After much persuasion, the woman agreed to forgive her sister. She called her sister on phone and announced that she had forgiven her. As soon as she did that, she became healed. She woke up the next day to discover that all the boils in her body had disappeared.

Un-forgiveness is one of the major hindrances to divine healing. The Spirit of God is ever willing to minister healing to people but the hardness caused by un-forgiveness will block the person's ability to receive it. Over the years we have seen folk failed to receive healing and deliverance just because they wouldn't let go of an offence committed against them.

Revenge is the spirit of the devil. The children of the world don't understand the idea of forgiveness. It makes look weak before the other person or your friends. The natural man is scared of being called weak.

Recently, a young man told me that he doesn't apologize because his father told him that it is only a weak person that keeps apologizing.

A lady told me that she would rather die than ask anyone to forgive her. She equally added that she can't be at peace until she had retaliated whatever offence committed against her. She said that no one offends her and gets away with it even if the person asks for forgiveness.

Another lady told me plainly that she does not forgive. She told me she still bears grudge against some people for over twenty years. She affirms that as long as the person who offended her is still alive, the battle hasn't ended.

Actually, that's the way of the natural man. The kingdom of God operates the exact opposite. Un-forgiveness is weakness; forgiveness is strength.

Although God is a sovereign God and can do what he wants, I believe that un-forgiveness will usually block healing. Forgiveness is a prerequisite for receiving healing. And I agree with that entirely.

In fact, un-forgiveness according to what Jesus said could even cost a person their salvation.

(Matthew 6:14-15 (NLT) 14 "If you forgive those who sin against you, your heavenly Father will forgive you. 15 But if you refuse to forgive others, your Father will not forgive your sins.

Our salvation is based on the truth that the father has forgiven us. Without being justified by God, we have no right to stand in His presence.

Hindrance #2 Un-Confessed Sin

Un-confessed sin is the biggest hindrances or obstacles to receiving healing and miracles. The Psalmist says; if I regard iniquity in my heart, the Lord will not hear me.

Un-confessed sin gives the devil a place to lurk around. That hidden sin becomes the chain with which the devil binds the one seeking healing and hinders him or her from receiving the miracle he or she seeks.

You see once the darkness is brought into the light, the father of darkness loses his power. So when sin is confessed and brought out into the open, the devil loses his power over us. And that is why that we must not let sin lurk around our lives. When we confess the sin, we become free afterwards. The devil loses his power and reason to oppress us.

If we confess our sin and receive forgiveness, there is absolutely nothing that will stop the gift of healing from manifesting.

Hindrance #3 – Healing Process

Sometimes it may seem like believers are not getting healed while unbelievers are, but I believe that when this seems to be the case, what is happening is that God is allowing the sickness to work something out in us.

So sometimes what may seem like a hindrance is actually just God's timing not matching what we think should be his timing. However, I have noticed that every Christian I know that has had to endure sickness for a while and then received their healing will testify that when they were through it they could see how God was working in their lives during the sickness. Healing can be instantaneous or gradual. God is not obligated to do things on our own terms. He does things on His own terms. Some people come to camp meetings and receive instant miracles while other notice their healing over time

We see this also in the ministry of Jesus. Blind Bathemus was instantly healed. The woman with the issue of blood healed the instant she touched the helm of Jesus' garment. The centurion had his servant healed the moment Jesus said go, your son will live. But then we see Jesus heal a blind man. He put His hand on the man's eyes and asked him if he saw anything. The man said he saw men walking about like trees. Jesus put his hand on the man's eyes a second time and the man could see clearly.

This shows that healing can be gradual. Some individuals miss it at this point because they stop believing if they can't see instant miracle. They conclude that God doesn't want to heal them and by so doing they terminate the healing process that had started.

Faith is to believe that you have received what you prayed for even when the answer hasn't manifested. When you pray for healing and it doesn't happen instantly, don't give up; the healing process has started. It may take a while but it sure will happen.

Some people had come to the prayer line for healing and discovered that they had been healed when they woke up the next day.

God may also decide to allow a process of healing just to bring you into some measure of awareness about the outworking of His power.

Kenneth Hagin Junior talked about how his son was sick and as a man of faith brought up by one of the greatest men of faith our world has ever known, he began to act by faith. He discovered that his son was not getting any better. He called his father and his father told him to switch to plan 'B'

Plan B is to take the boy to the hospital. He was surprised that his father, Kenneth Hagin Senior, a man of great faith could suggest going to the hospital. He obeyed and the boy was taken to the hospital.

The boy was taken to the theater for operation. During the operation, a nurse confessed that she had been touched by God. A lot of testimonies emanated from that admission at the hospital.

God is not stereotyped; He can move anyhow He wants. Our responsibility is to follow Him. God can decide to heal you as you continue to take your medication according to your doctor's prescription.

I don't believe God will ever deliberately cause sickness to come upon any of his children, but when it does come through natural causes or through our own sin, he can still use our sickness to accomplish something in us or to reach out to other people in such a way as we would otherwise not be willing to deal with.

#4 God is Using My Sickness to Teach Me a Lesson

Most people that God is using their sickness to teach them lessons. The irony of the whole case is that such people never seem to grasp the lesson God is trying to teach them. If you ask them what the lesson is about, you will discover that they can't tell what the lesson is about.

Jesus came to give us life in abundance. Sickness and diseases are not part of abundant life. Sickness is of the devil. It came as a result of man's fall.

Sickness is an instrument of the devil. I don't understand how God will use that which belongs to the devil to teach his children lesson. He has given us the Holy Spirit to be our teacher. The Holy Spirit guides us into all truth about our salvation, our fellowship with the father, the finished work of our lord Jesus Christ

Healing is part of our redemption package. Isaiah 53 tells that the Messiah took our sin and sicknesses. Mathew confirms that in chapter 8 verse 17 that Jesus took our infirmities and carried our sicknesses.

Hindrance #4 – Lack of Persistence

There is a place of persistence if we need healing from God. We know and have see God perfecting the healing of individuals instantaneously; we have also seen where healing takes a gradual process.

Naaman was asked by Prophet Elisha to dip himself in Jordan River seven times. Healing was not evident until he had dipped the seventh time. If he wasn't persistent, his healing wouldn't have been perfected.

Although our teaching of faith is that we don't keep asking God for a particular thing since would look like we didn't believe he heard us the first time we prayed, but we need to understand that the bible also teaches persistence in prayer and faith.

We could get confused if we don't take the time ti decipher between the Biblical teaching on faith and persistence in prayer.

There is a line here that can be a bit confusing. On one side of the divide is praying about something, (like healing or the salvation of a loved one or even the fruit of the womb) and believing God has heard us and so will act on our prayers.

The idea here is that if we continue to pray about something we are expressing a lack of faith in our previous prayers. If we believe God hears and answers our prayers then don't have to keep asking because it shows a lack of faith in God.

This kind of reasoning is understandable and can even be supported or back it up with some scripture, but we also know there is the teaching of our Lord Jesus Christ on the other side of the line that says we have to persist in prayer. There're at least two places in the gospel where Jesus makes it clear that we should persist in prayers.

As Jesus was rounding off his teaching on what we call the Lord's prayer in Luke 11 He goes on to teach us about persistence in prayer in Luke 11 5-9, let's have a look at that…

(Luke 11:5-9 (NLT) 5 Then, teaching them more about prayer, he used this story: "Suppose you went to a friend's house at midnight, wanting to borrow three loaves of bread. You say to him, 6 'A friend of mine has just arrived for a visit, and I have nothing for him to eat.' 7 And suppose he calls out from his bedroom, 'Don't bother me. The door is locked for the night, and my family and I are all in bed. I can't help you.' 8 But I tell you this—though he won't do it for friendship's sake, if you keep knocking long enough, he will get up and give you whatever you need because of your shameless persistence. 9 "And so I tell you, keep on asking, and you will receive what you ask for. Keep on seeking, and you will find. Keep on knocking, and the door will be opened to you.

As you can clearly see here, a lack of shameless persistence to keep on asking could be a valid hindrance to our healing. This can apply on the part of the person needing the healing and likewise to the person who is ministering healing to the sick.

Jesus teaches the same lesson with the parable of the persistent widow in Luke 18 who pestered a slack judge until he got so sick of her asking for justice that he granted her what she wanted.

The point here is that persistence should be in faith. We should hold on to the word of God that promises us healing. Our prayer during the time we expect our healing to be perfected shouldn't be in doubt. We shouldn't repeat what we have prayed for as though God did not hear or answer us the first time.

This brings us to the difference between asking God for healing and demanding the perfection of our healing in the name of Jesus Christ.

So, after you have prayed or have been prayed for, don't come back the next day and say: God, I asked you for healing the other day but you didn't heal me; please heal me today Lord. Or I have been standing in this line receiving prayers and ministration but nothing is working. Please God let it work today.

When you pray like that or have such mindset about healing, you are not likely to get healed because you are expressing doubt not faith.

Jesus says in mark 11:23, 24 whatsoever you desire, when you pray, believe that you already have it and it shall be yours.

Hindrance #5 – Unbelief

Unbelief is a state of not being sure that our prayers will be answered. We all at some point are hit with this wave of unbelief. From time to time we are all faced with some form of unbelief.

Sometimes we waver when we look at the size of our problem. We are more comfortable or disposed to believing God when we think the challenge is small.

I have established earlier in this book that God considers unbelief an affront on His personality. I said that God is pleased when we demonstrate our trust in Him. He acts within the limits we allow Him in our situation. God is not limited in His capacity or ability to do anything. The Bibles tell us that nothing is impossible with our God. But Jesus also tells us that nothing is impossible to him who believes.

Let's go back to the story of the man who brought his demon possessed child to the disciples to Jesus to be healed. I believe that in some way most of us can identify with that desperate father with a sick child when he asked Jesus if he could heal his boy in Mark 9. The man pleaded with Jesus to do something if he could and Jesus replied:

(Mark 9:23-24 (NLT) 23 "What do you mean, 'If I can'?" Jesus asked. "Anything is possible if a person believes." 24 The father instantly cried out, "I do believe, but help me overcome my unbelief!"

Jesus threw the responsibility back to the man. It's up to you if your child gets healed or not. The question is not whether God is able.

The question is whether you are able to draw from God's ability this ever flowing.

I will relate the healing power of God to electric current. The current is ever flowing. Power is available. The question is whether you have electricity in your house. If you don't have electricity in your house or in any of your gadgets, it's not because power is not available; it's because something is wrong with your connection. So, the right thing to do is to check your connection to rectify whatever is wrong.

CNN is on air twenty-four hours. If for any reason you can't access the channel on your TV set, the fault won't be from CNN especially when others are getting the station; you have to check your antenna.

That's exactly what Jesus was trying to explain to the man. The power of God is ever available. It's unbelief that can disconnect you from it.

Yes we believe but sometimes a measure of unbelief can creep in and when it does, you can be sure that such unbelief can become a hindrance to the flow of God's power when you need healing.

Nothing blocks the flow of supernatural power like unbelief. Satan can't hinder God from healing you. The enormity of your sickness is not a factor before God. The most powerful blocker to receiving the supernatural power of God in your life is unbelief. Even Jesus himself was hindered by people's unbelief?

Jesus could not do much miracles in His home town because His people only saw him as the carpenter, the son of Mary and so they refused to believe in His ability to do miracles.

As far as the people of his home town were concerned, Jesus was no one special and so they refused accept he could help them.

Listen to what Jesus said about them

(Mark 6:4-6 (NLT) 4 Then Jesus told them, "A prophet is honored everywhere except in his own hometown and among his relatives and his own family." 5 And because of their unbelief, he couldn't do any mighty miracles among them except to place his hands on a few sick people and heal them.

Think about it, even Jesus himself was restricted by people's unbelief. Unbelief is such a big hindrance that it stopped even Jesus from doing what he normally does? The power of God does not flow in the atmosphere of unbelief.

If you need healing and you also full of doubt or unbelief, then you must first deal with your unbelief before praying for your healing. That is not how God wants us to approach people who need healing. Without faith we cannot please God and if we are not pleasing him it's unlikely He will work for us.

Jesus says in Mark 16 17, 18 that these signs shall follow them that believe. ... They will be able to place their hands on the sick, and they will be healed."

Notice that the signs He mentioned are to follow only those who believe not those who don't or those who are in need of the signs.

You don't access the power of god because you are in pain, you do because you believe

(Mark 16:18 ... They will be able to place their hands on the sick, and they will be healed."

Ignorance of the Character of God!

Many people are ignorant of the character of God - many Christians are not familiar with the nature and the will of their loving Heavenly Father. If you don't understand the loving nature of our heavenly father; the fact that God is love, and that He gives only good things to His children, you may not be able to receive your healing (I Jn.4:7-8).

1Jo 4:7 Beloved, let us love one another: for love is of God; and every one that loveth is born of God, and knoweth God. {is born: Gr. has been born}

8 He that loveth not knoweth not God; for God is love.

(KJV)

You can know the character of God by looking at Jesus. Jesus, in His earthly life, was the personification of the character of God. He reflected the nature of our heavenly father in every ramification. He continually demonstrated the will of God by healing the sick. When he healed the sick, he revealed to us the heart of the father. He told His disciples that anyone who has seen Him has seen the father. In other words, the father will not do anything different from what I am doing.

Jesus in His earthly ministry promoted healing as God's will for humanity. The Word of God promotes healing from cover to cover. But many Christians don't understand that healing is included in the work of redemption. Some see healing as a special favor granted to those who are destined to get it.

You are better disposed to receive your healing if you understand that it is part of the redemption package. God included healing in the finished work of His son. Ignorance of basic faith principles and the healing Scriptures will delay healing.

It is important for us to constantly listen to and study the Truths of the Word of God. Yes, the world is full of sickness and disease, but we don't have to be partakers or accept it as ours. The word of God declares we have been redeemed from the curse of sickness and disease and that is a higher truth and reality than the reality of the presence of disease in our world. Jesus told us that it is the thief (Satan) who came to steal, kill, and destroy. Jesus said that He came to give us abundant life and things pertaining to life (Jn.10:10).

Sickness is not part of the abundant life Jesus came to give us. When you are armed with such knowledge, resisting sickness and disease will be easy for you.

Chapter Five

Healing Scriptures

The word of God is life; it brings healing and sound health to the body. When you allow what God has said concerning your healing to flow into your heart the healing power will flow into your body and you will see the physical evidence in your body. Our entire lives are transformed when we allow God's word to come alive in our hearts.

1 No plague shall come near your dwelling (Ps. 91:10).

2 I will strengthen you upon the bed of languishing; I will turn all your bed in your sickness (Ps. 41:3).
3 You shall be buried in a good old age (Gen. 15:15).
4. You shall come to your grave in a full age like as a shock of corn cometh in its season (Job 5:26).
5 Ps 103:3 Who forgiveth all thine iniquities; who healeth all thy diseases

6. I will take sickness away from the midst of you and the number of your days I will fulfill (Ex. 23:25, 26).

7. As your days, so shall your strength be (Deut. 33:25).
"

8 Heal me, O Lord, and I will be healed; save me and I will be saved, for you are the one I

praise." ~ **Jeremiah** 17:14

9. *De 23:5 Nevertheless the LORD thy God would not hearken unto Balaam; but the LORD thy God turned the curse into a blessing unto thee, because the LORD thy God loved thee.*

10 He said, "If you listen carefully to the LORD your God and do what is right in his eyes, if you pay attention to his commands and keep all his decrees, I will not bring on you any of the diseases I brought on the Egyptians, for I am the LORD, who heals you."
~ Exodus 15:26

11 *Ga 3:13 Christ hath redeemed us from the curse of the law, being made a curse for us: for it is written, Cursed is every one that hangeth on a tree:*

12. *I will not put any of the diseases you are afraid of on you, but I will take all sickness*

away from you (Deut. 7:15).

13. As your days, so shall your strength be (Deut. 33:25).
14 Job 33:24,25 Then he is gracious unto him, and saith, Deliver him from going down to the pit: I have found a ransom. {a ransom: or, an atonement}

His flesh shall be fresher than a child's: he shall return to the days of his youth: {a child's: Heb. childhood}.

15 I have healed you and brought up your soul from the grave; I have kept you alive from going down into the pit (Ps. 30:1, 2).
16. I will give you strength and bless you with peace (Ps. 29:11).
17. I will preserve you and keep you alive (Ps. 41:2).
18. You shall be buried in a good old age (Gen. 15:15).

19. I am the health of your countenance and your God (Ps.43:5).
20. 1. I am the Lord that healeth thee (Ex. 15:26).
21. I will satisfy you with long life (Ps. 91:16).
22. When I see the blood, I will pass over you and the plague shall not be upon you to destroy you (Ex. 12:13).

23. I sent My word and healed you and delivered you from your destructions (Ps. 107:20).
24. You shall not die, but live, and declare My works (Ps. 118:17).
25. I heal your broken heart and bind up your wounds (Ps. 147:3).
26. The years of your life shall be many (Pr. 4:10).
27. Trusting Me brings health to your navel and marrow to your bones (Pr. 3:8).
28. My words are life to you, and health/medicine to all your flesh (Pr. 4:22).

29. Pr 15:30 *The light of the eyes rejoiceth the heart: and a good report maketh the bones fat.* (KJV)

30. Prov. 16:24 *Pleasant words are as an honeycomb, sweet to the soul, and health to the bones.* (KJV)

31. Pr 17:22 *A merry heart doeth good like a medicine: but a broken spirit drieth the bones. {like: or, to}*

(KJV) 29. The eyes of the blind shall be opened. The eyes of them that see shall not be dim (Isa.32:3; 35:5).
32. The ears of the deaf shall be unstopped. The ears of them that hear shall hearken (Isa. 32:3; 35:5).
33. The tongue of the dumb shall sing. The tongue of the stammerers shall be ready to speak plainly (Isa. 35:6; 32:4).
34. The lame man shall leap as a hart (Isa. 35:6).

35. I will recover you and make you to live. I am ready to save you (Isa. 38:16, 20).
36. I give power to the faint. I increase strength to them that have no might (Isa. 40:29).
37. I will renew your strength. I will strengthen and help you (Isa. 40:31; 41:10).
38. To your old age and gray hairs I will carry you and I will deliver you (Isa. 46:4).
39. I bore your sickness (Isa. 53:4).
40. I carried your pains (Isa. 53:4).
41. I was put to sickness for you (Isa. 53:10).
42. With My stripes you are healed (Isa. 53:5).
43. I will heal you (Isa. 57:19).
44. Your light shall break forth as the morning and your health shall spring forth speedily (Isa. 58:8).
45. I will restore health unto you, and I will heal you of your wounds saith the Lord (Jer. 30:17).

46. Behold I will bring it health and cure, and I will cure you, and will reveal unto you the abundance of peace and truth (Jer. 33:6).
47. I will bind up that which was broken and will strengthen that which was sick (Eze. 34:16).
48. Behold, I will cause breath to enter into you and you shall live. And I shall put My Spirit in you and you shall live (Eze. 37:5, 14).
49. Whithersoever the rivers shall come shall live. They shall be healed and everything shall live where the river comes (Eze. 47:9).
50. Seek Me and you shall live (Amos 5:4, 6).
51. Mal 4:2 But unto you that fear my name shall the Sun of righteousness arise with healing in his wings; and ye shall go forth, and grow up as calves of the stall. (KJV)
52. I will, be thou clean (Mt. 8:3).
53. He took our infirmities (Mt. 8:17).
54. He bore our sicknesses (Mt. 8:17).
55. Ex 15:26 And said, If thou wilt diligently

hearken to the voice of the LORD thy God, and wilt do that which is right in his sight, and wilt give ear to his commandments, and keep all his statutes, I will put none of these diseases upon thee, which I have brought upon the Egyptians: for I am the LORD that healeth thee.

56. Mt 14:14 And Jesus went forth, and saw a great multitude, and was moved with compassion toward them, and he healed their sick.(KJV)

57. I heal all manner of sickness and all manner of disease (Mt. 4:23).

58. According to your faith, be it unto you (Mt. 9:29).

59. I give you power and authority over all unclean spirits to cast them out, and to heal all manner of sickness and all manner of disease (Mt. 10:1 & Lk. 9:1).

60. Mt 12:15 But when Jesus knew it, he withdrew himself from thence: and great multitudes followed him, and he healed them all;

61. *As many as touch Me are made perfectly whole (Mt. 14:36).*
62. *Healing is the children's bread (Mt. 15:26).*
63. *I do all things well. I make the deaf to hear and the dumb to speak (Mk. 7:37).*
64. *If you can believe, all things are possible to him that believeth (Mk. 9:23; 11:23, 24).*
65. *They shall lay hands on the sick and they shall recover (Mk. 16:18).*
66. *My anointing heals the brokenhearted, and delivers the captives, recovers sight to the blind, and sets at liberty those that are bruised (Lk. 4:18; Isa. 10:27; 61:1).*
67. *Lk. 9:11 And the people, when they knew it, followed him: and he received them, and spake unto them of the kingdom of God, and healed them that had need of healing (KJV)*

68. Lu 9:56 *For the Son of man is not come to destroy men's lives, but to save them. And they went to another village.*
69. *Behold, I give you authority over all the enemy's power and nothing shall by any means hurt you* (Lk. 10:19).
70. Lu 13:16 *And ought not this woman, being a daughter of Abraham, whom Satan hath bound, lo, these eighteen years, be loosed from this bond on the sabbath day?*
71. *In Me is life* (Jn. 1:4).
72. *I am the bread of life. I give you life* (Jn. 6:33, 35).
73. *The words I speak unto you are spirit and life* (Jn. 6:63).
74. *I am come that you might have life, and that you might have it more abundantly* (Jn. 10:10).
75. *I am the resurrection and the life* (Jn. 11:25).
76. *If you ask anything in My name, I will do*

it (Jn. 14:14).
77. Faith in My name makes you strong and gives you perfect soundness (Acts 3:16).
78. Ac 4:30 By stretching forth thine hand to heal; and that signs and wonders may be done by the name of thy holy child Jesus.
79. Jesus Christ, make you whole (Acts 9:34).
80. Ac 10:38 How God anointed Jesus of Nazareth with the Holy Ghost and with power: who went about doing good, and healing all that were oppressed of the devil; for God was with him.
81. Ac 19:12 So that from his body were brought unto the sick handkerchiefs or aprons, and the diseases departed from them, and the evil spirits went out of them.
82. The law of the Spirit of life in Me has made you free from the law of sin and death (Rom. 8:2).
83. The same Spirit that raised Me from the dead now lives in you and that Spirit will

quicken your mortal body (Rom. 8:11). 84. 1Co 6:15 Know ye not that your bodies are the members of Christ? shall I then take the members of Christ, and make them the members of an harlot? God forbid. 85. Your body is the temple of My Spirit and you're to glorify God in your body (I Cor. 6:19, 20). 86) And a woman was there who had been crippled by a spirit for eighteen years. She was bent over and could not straighten up at all. When Jesus saw her, he called her forward and said to her, "Woman, you are set free from your infirmity." Then he put his hands on her, and immediately she straightened up and praised God. **Luke 13:11-13**

87. He said to her, "Daughter, your faith has healed you. Go in peace and be freed from your suffering. **Mark 5:34**

*88. My life may be made manifest in your mortal flesh (II Cor. 4:10, 11).
89. I have delivered you from death, I do deliver you, and if you trust Me I will yet deliver you (II Cor. 1:10).
90. I have given you My name and have put all things under your feet (Eph. 1:21, 22).
91. I want it to be well with you and I want you to live long on the earth. (Eph. 6:3).
92. I have delivered you from the authority of darkness (Col. 1:13).
93. I will deliver you from every evil work (II Tim. 4:18).
94. I tasted death for you. I destroyed the devil who had the power of death. I've delivered you from the fear of death and bondage (Heb. 2:9, 14, 15).
95. Lift up the weak hands and the feeble knees. Don't let that which is lame be turned aside but rather let Me heal it (Heb. 12:12, 13).*

96. Let the elders anoint you and pray for you in My name and I will raise you up (Jas. 5:14,15).

97. Pray for one another and I will heal you (Jas. 5:16).

98. By My stripes you were healed (I Pet. 2:24).

99. My Divine power has given unto you all things that pertain unto life and godliness through the knowledge of Me (II Pet. 1:3).

100 Whosoever will, let him come and take of the water of life freely (Rev. 22:17).

101. Beloved, I wish above all things that you may...be in health (3 John 2).

Chapter Six

PRAYING WITH THE SCRIPTURES

This chapter is about how to pray with the scriptures. A lot of people don't know how to do that. Prayer becomes an empty noise when it is not backed up by God's word. The word of God gives force to your prayer. God only responds to His word; consequently, your plea and cry will miss the mark if they don't carry the substance of God's promises.

When you come to a court of law, you are required to tender your evidence and back up your case with the constitution of the government of your country. If you cannot back up your case with the constitution, you are going to lose the case. No judge will listen to empty plea. It's worst when you plead ignorance. It is said that ignorance is not an excuse in the court of law.

You obtain result in spiritual things by standing on God's word. So, if you want to be healed, you must know what the word says about healing. You don't obtain healing because you think it's unfair for you to suffer from a particular ailment for many years. Actually, God doesn't care about that. The intensity of your pain doesn't attract divine pity. Your ability to stand on God's promises is what attracts divine power.

It has been said that God does not have sentiment, He operates by principles. If we neglect His principles, we will be consumed with our problems.

Let me give you three basic principles that will enable you obtain results through God's word.

1# Hear the Word

Ro 10:17 So then faith cometh by hearing, and hearing by the word of God. (KJV)

Pr 4:1 Hear, ye children, the instruction of a father, and attend to know understanding.

Math.8:24 Therefore whosoever heareth these sayings of mine, and doeth them, I will liken him unto a wise man, which built his house upon a rock:

These potions of the scriptures emphasize the importance of listening to God's word. The first step to an effective use of God's word is to hear it.

To hear means more than having a sound filter in to your ears as you are relaxing of just passing by. It means a deliberate and conscious attention to a body of knowledge as to how you deliberately go out of your way to listen to someone who shares the information needed to improve on your job or business.

We are admonished to pay close attention to God's word. Paul tells us in Romans 10:17 that faith comes by hearing God's word. Your faith is built as you keep attending to the word.

Make a conscious effort to listen to teachings on healing and deliverance. The more you do that, the more your understanding of healing grows and the more your faith develops. When this happens, you are sure of receiving your healing.

There is a story of the healing of a cripple in Acts 14. The story shows us how faith leaps up in our heart as we listen to God's word.

Acts 14:7-10 And there they preached the gospel.

And there sat a certain man at Lystra, impotent in his feet, being a cripple from his mother's womb, who never had walked:

The same heard Paul speak: who steadfastly beholding him, and perceiving that he had faith to be healed, Said with a loud voice, Stand upright on thy feet. And he leaped and walked.

Notice that Paul first preached the gospel. Faith comes by hearing God's word.

While Paul was preaching, the cripple was listening. The more he listened, the more he became convinced that healing was his. Paul saw that the word has produced faith in the man and commanded him to stand up. The man immediately responded to Paul's command because he was already waiting for that.

When you listen to God's word, your faith will come alive and miracle is certain.

3#Speak the Word

The next step in activating God's creative power is to speak the word. Healing can't become a reality in your life until you claim it. The way to claim your healing or any spiritual blessing is to declare that it is yours.

The scriptures confirm that God has given us all things that pertains to life and godliness. We already have all that we need. God has made good everything available to us through the death and resurrection of His son Jesus Christ. All things are yours. Healing is yours. Deliverance is yours. All spiritual blessings are ours for the taking.

In the mind of God, you are healed, delivered from the powers of darkness and translated into light. Actually, God is surprised when we complain about sickness, lack or any other thing that the finished work of Jesus has made available to us. It's like your little daughter crying for hunger when the house is filled with what to eat and drink. Your answer to her would be: sweet heart, check the fridge and take whatever you want.

We transfer healing and deliverance from the realm of the spirit into our body is the word. You must not close your mouth when you need healing, deliverance or any spiritual blessing.

God told Joshua not to allow the book of the law to depart out of his mouth. Joshua was to meditate on it day and night. The word meditate, actually means to mutter or to speak to yourself as in soliloquy.

Jos 1:8 This book of the law shall not depart out of thy mouth; but thou shalt meditate therein day and night, that thou mayest observe to do according to all that is written therein: for then thou shalt make thy way prosperous, and then thou shalt have good success. {have...: or, do wisely}

(KJV)

The result of speaking the word to yourself as we see in the case of Joshua is that you will make your way prosperous and have good success. Simply put; you will obtain the result you seek.

The word of declares that Jesus took our infirmity and carried our sickness. So, you go ahead and confess: Jesus has taken my infirmity and carried my sickness. I refuse to suffer from the sickness or disease that has already been borne away. I command you disease/sickness (name the disease) to leave my body right now in the mighty name of Jesus.

Act on the Word

The third way to activate God's creative power is to act on the word. Acting on the word means to do what the word says.

Jesus tells us that those who believe shall lay hand on the sick and the sick shall recover. Do you believe? Then do what the word says. Lay hands on any sick person around you. Don't forget that you're also a person. Lay hands on yourself and command any sickness or disease in your body to leave right away.

I have mentioned earlier that God has given us everything we need to live a happy and fulfilled life. Our salvation package is complete. Even men and women under the old covenant knew what an awesome salvation God has made available for us. The Psalmist mentioned these benefits.

Psalms 103:2 Bless the LORD, O my soul, and forget not all his benefits:

3 Who forgiveth all thine iniquities; who healeth all thy diseases;

4 Who redeemeth thy life from destruction; who crowneth thee with lovingkindness and tender mercies;

5 Who satisfieth thy mouth with good things; so that thy youth is renewed like the eagle's.

Do you notice that the Psalmist said that God has healed all our diseases?

Many people believe that God forgives sin but they don't believe He heals sicknesses and diseases. The same verse of the scripture that tells us that we have been forgiven also tells us that we have been healed.

Jesus paid for your healing the same time He paid for your sin. You're losing out of the whole package if you accept forgiveness without accepting healing. Healing is as much yours as forgiveness of sin is. And the interesting thing is that it takes the same act of faith to receive forgiveness as it takes to receive healing. You don't need a higher faith or anointing to receive your healing, just accept that you are healed as you have accepted that you have been forgiven. Proclaim it and don't allow anything whatsoever to stop you from declaring that you are healed

The Woman with the Issue of Blood

Mark 5:25 And a certain woman, which had an issue of blood twelve years,

26 And had suffered many things of many physicians, and had spent all that she had, and was nothing bettered, but rather grew worse,

27 When she had heard of Jesus, came in the press behind, and touched his garment.

28 For she said, If I may touch but his clothes, I shall be whole.

29 And straightway the fountain of her blood was dried up; and she felt in her body that she was healed of that plague.

30 And Jesus, immediately knowing in himself that virtue had gone out of him, turned him about in the press, and said, Who touched my clothes?

31 And his disciples said unto him, Thou seest the multitude thronging thee, and sayest thou, Who touched me?

32 And he looked round about to see her that had done this thing.

33 But the woman fearing and trembling, knowing what was done in her, came and fell down before him, and told him all the truth.

34 And he said unto her, Daughter, thy faith hath made thee whole; go in peace, and be whole of thy plague.

Mark opened the story of this woman by telling us how much and how long she had suffered. The duration of her sickness was twelve years. The nature of the sickness was unusual. The intensity of the sickness was high. She was on a danger list as far as health is concern. There's something more; she had enriched many doctors in the process of trying to get well. So, we can safely assume that her pocket was running dry at this point in her life.

Perhaps, your situation is like that or even worse than this woman's; don't give up; your miracle is as sure as that of this woman the day she met Jesus.

I want you to pay attention to how this woman got her miracle; repeat exactly what she did and your own miracle will also materialize.

Experts have told us that if we study what someone else has done and repeat exactly the same thing with the same attitude and determination, we will get the result that that person got.

So let's look at what this woman did. Actually, she combined the three principles I've mentioned above

First of all, she heard about Jesus.

27 When she had heard of Jesus, came in the press behind, and touched his

garment.

Notice that she didn't take any step until she had heard about Jesus.

Have you heard about Jesus? If you haven't heard about Jesus Christ, let me tell you about Him.

He is the Son of the living God who came into the world to save humanity from sin and the dominion of Satan. He came to reconcile man back to God after man had been separated from God because of the disobedience of Adam and Eve back in the Garden of Eden.

He sacrificed His life on the cross of Calvary so that you and I can become free and able to stand in the presence of the God of the whole universe. He became our substitute so that we can become the righteousness of God in Him.

2Co 5:21 For he hath made him to be sin for us, who knew no sin; that we might be made the righteousness of God in him. (KJV)

His suffering and death did not only bring us forgiveness and righteousness, it brings healing and wholeness to us.

1Pe 2:24 Who his own self bare our sins in his own body on the tree, that we, being dead to sins, should live unto righteousness: by whose stripes ye were healed. {on: or, to}

Mt 8:16 When the even was come, they brought unto him many that were possessed with devils: and he cast out the spirits with his word, and healed all that were sick:

17 That it might be fulfilled which was spoken by Esaias the prophet, saying, Himself took our infirmities, and bare our sicknesses.

Well, there're so many things to say about Jesus. We will continue that in other books. But suffice to know that Jesus died to set you free from sin, sickness and Satan.

So, this woman heard about Jesus. What did she hear about Jesus that interested her?

You know that people more often than not listen to something that addresses their pressing need. So, I suppose the woman must have heard about the Jesus who went about healing people and setting men and women free from all kinds of bondages.

Now, stop whatever you are doing and go listen to messages on healing. Stop listening to the statistics of the spread of corona virus. Stop listening to how many people who have died from the disease. Listen to healing messages. Listen to what the Bible says concerning your health.

She said to herself

The second thing this woman did was to speak to herself.

28 For she said, If I may touch but his clothes, I shall be whole.

Actually, the real interpretation of that scripture is: for she kept saying to herself, once I touch his clothes, I will be healed. She didn't say it once. She kept saying it.

I can imagine her saying; today is my day. I've suffered enough. All I need is an opportunity to get close to Him; once I do, it will all over. I refuse to spend another day with blood flowing all over me. The last hospital bill I paid to those doctors is the last they will get from me. Everything is ending today and right here, right now.

What do you say about your case? Are you saying, let's hope they will find the vaccine. Our medical experts are working very hard; I'm sure they will come up with something any time soon.

That shouldn't be your confession. Don't wait for vaccine; take the one that is already provided. Jesus has already given us the vaccine against any kind of sickness. This vaccine is more than one thousand percent guaranteed. Go for it.

The good thing about the healing power of God is that you can activate it right where you are. You don't need a doctor to make it work. You don't even need a deliverance or healing minister (it's okay if you have any of them around). Just continue to confess your healing like the woman in our case study did

She Acted

The third thing this woman did was to act on her confession. She confessed that she would be made whole if she touched Jesus' clothes and she went ahead to do as she had said.

27 When she had heard of Jesus, came in the press behind, and touched his garment.

She touched the master's garment and she was healed. If she didn't complete this third step, maybe she might not have been healed.

Some people only stop at the first two steps. They hear God's word, they say it to themselves but fail to act on it.

To act on the word means to do the word says to do.

They shall lay hands on the sick and the sick shall recover. That is God's word; so you go ahead and lay your hands on that sick person around you and pray for them.

Well, you will say John I'm the one who needs healing.

Well, the last time I checked you were a human being and the last time I looked up that scripture in Mark 16:18, it didn't say it must be another person. It simply says you shall lay hands on anyone who is sick and that person will recover. So, can you now see that you can lay your hand on your- self and expect the same result?

Another way to act on the word is not agree with any contrary evidence that you feel. The word is true irrespective of our feeling. You may still feel very sick after your confession and prayers but you must learn that the kingdom of God doesn't work with feeling.

Settle it in your heart that you are healed and you will eventually see the physical manifestation of your confession.

A Unique Model

Jesus gave us a perfect model of getting answer from God in Mark 11, 23-24

Mark 11:23 For verily I say unto you, That whosoever shall say unto this mountain, Be thou removed, and be thou cast into the sea; and shall not doubt in his heart, but shall believe that those things which he saith shall come to pass; he shall have whatsoever he saith.

24 Therefore I say unto you, What things soever ye desire, when ye pray, believe that ye receive them, and ye shall have them. (KJV)

You see, what Jesus is saying here is simple. When you speak or pray about anything, just believe that God has answered and quit trying to figure out the process. Don't waste your time trying to figure out how the answer will come; just believe that it's done.

I know it could be somehow hard especially when we are dealing with sickness. The symptoms shout so loud that you'll wonder if you're actually healed. That is exactly what the devil lays hands on to rob many of their healing.

Suppose you went to the hospital for a routine check up and the doctor told you that you've got cancer, what would be your reaction?

You've never felt the symptom of any sickness yet a qualified and reputable doctor tells you you've got a disease. You'd go home from that hospital not just believing but knowing for sure that you have a disease. You'll even start telling your friends and loved ones that you've got cancer. Why? Because the doctor said so and you believe him!

You see, human beings believe more in sickness and disease than they believe in divine healing.

When you pray for healing believe that you are healed. Why? Because the word of God says so!

The same way you leave that doctor's office being so sure of the disease in your body even when you've never felt the pain, so also you should be sure that you're already healed whether you feel relieved instantly or not.

Now let's take few scriptures from the hundred healing scriptures above and turn them into prayer and confession.

Faith Proclamation 1

Col.1:12 Giving thanks unto the Father, which hath made us meet to be partakers of the inheritance of the saints in light:

13 Who hath delivered us from the power of darkness, and hath translated us into the kingdom of his dear Son: {his...: Gr. the Son of his love}

14 In whom we have redemption through his blood, even the forgiveness of sins: (KJV)

I give thanks to the father who has qualified me through His so Jesus Christ to partake of the inheritance of the saints in light. I have been delivered from the dominion of darkness, sin, sickness and death and I have been translated into the kingdom of His dear son. I have been redeemed by the precious blood of Jesus Christ from the bondage of the devil.

Today I declare that I am free from sin, sickness and Satan. I belong to the family of God where there is no sickness, disease and devil. The authority and dominion of darkness has ended in my life. No more will I be afflicted, buffeted and harassed by disease or demonic forces in Jesus name. the power of sickness and disease is broken over my life

Faith Proclamation 2

Mt 8:16 When the even was come, they brought unto him many that were possessed with devils: and he cast out the spirits with his word, and healed all that were sick:

17 That it might be fulfilled which was spoken by Esaias the prophet, saying, Himself took our infirmities, and bare our sicknesses.

Jesus has taken my infirmities and borne my sicknesses. The reign of sickness, pain and disease has ended in my life. He bore them so that I will bear them no more. Therefore I am free. I am healed. I am delivered.

I refuse to suffer for what has already been paid for. It is an abomination for me to pay for what has already been paid for. Jesus paid for it so that I may enjoy the benefits. Therefore, I claim my healing right now in the name of Jesus Christ.

Faith proclamation 3

"While Jesus was still speaking, someone came from the house of Jairus, the synagogue leader. "Your daughter is dead," he said. "Don't bother the teacher anymore." Hearing this, Jesus said to Jairus, "Don't be afraid; just believe, and she will be healed." When he arrived at the house of Jairus, he did not let anyone go in with him except Peter, John and James, and the child's father and mother. Meanwhile, all the people were wailing and mourning for her. "Stop wailing," Jesus said. "She is not dead but asleep." They laughed at him, knowing that she was dead. But he took her by the. hand and said, "My child, get up!" Her spirit returned, and at once she stood up. Then Jesus told them to give her something to eat. Her parents were astonished, but he

ordered them not to tell anyone what had happened." ~ Luke 8:49-56

I am not afraid because I believe. It doesn't matter what doctors or experts have said about my case. I rise from my bed of sickness and affliction. My body is the temple of the Holy Spirit. God lives in me. My father who lives in me is greater than all. No power will be able to snatch me out of His hands. I am a partaker of God's divine nature. I have the authority of the name of Jesus. I refuse to allow the devil to disease on me. I declare complete healing and soundness from the crown of my head to the soul of feet.

Chapter Seven

Seven Days Prayer Journal for Healing and Deliverance

In this chapter, we shall journey together to perfect your healing and deliverance. God said to children of Israel, what I hear you say in my ear that will I do unto you. In other words, God will permit to receive what your mouth has uttered.

I want you to this prayer appointment for the next seven days. You will say the prayer points three time daily-morning afternoon and evening.

Day One

*But I will restore you to health and heal your wounds,' declares the LORD" ~ **Jeremiah 30:17***

- I cancel my name, my family and Ministry from the death register, with the fire of God, in the name of Jesus.
- Every inherited sickness in my life, depart from me now, in the name of Jesus.
- Every evil water in my body, dry up and get out, in the name of Jesus
- I refuse to get used to ill health, in the name of Jesus.
- Every door open to infirmity in my life, be permanently closed today, in the name of Jesus

- *Every power contenting with God in my life, be roasted, in the name of Jesus.*
- *I stand against every evil covenant of sudden death, in the name of Jesus.*
- *I break every conscious and unconscious evil covenant of untimely death, in the name of Jesus.*
- *You spirit of death and hell, you have no document in my life, in the name of Jesus.*
- *You stones of death, depart from my ways, in the name of Jesus.*

Day Two

But he was pierced for our transgressions, he was crushed for our iniquities; the punishment that brought us peace was on him, and by his wounds we are healed."
~ Isaiah 53:4-5

- You evil current of death, lose your grip over my life, in the name of Jesus.
- No evil will touch me throughout my life, in the name of Jesus.
- Let the power to be in good health throughout the days of my life fall upon me, in the name of Jesus.

- Every area of my life that is at the point of death, receive the touch of revival, in the name of Jesus.
- Throughout the days of my life, I will not be a candidate for incurable disease, in the name of Jesus.
- Every stubborn and prayer resisting sickness, loose your evil hold upon my life, in the name of Jesus.
- *Let the blood of Jesus flush out every inherited satanic deposit of sicknesses from my system in Jesus mighty name.*
- *I release myself from the grip of any sickness or disease transferred into my life from my mother's womb in Jesus name*
- *Let the blood of Jesus wash away any germ, bacteria or virus from my system in Jesus name*

- *I break and lose myself from every inherited evil covenant of sickness and disease in Jesus name*

Day Three

Ex 15:26 And said, If thou wilt diligently hearken to the voice of the LORD thy God, and wilt do that which is right in his sight, and wilt give ear to his commandments, and keep all his statutes, I will put none of these diseases upon thee, which I have brought upon the Egyptians: for I am the LORD that healeth thee.

- *Father Lord, let my intestine and every organ of my body experience the fireworks of the Holy Ghost, in Jesus name.*

- *Father Lord, let there be a disassociation between my body and the evil food I have eaten, in the name of Jesus.*
- *Father Lord, in the name of Jesus, I vomit every evil food that I have eaten.*
- *Let the blood of Jesus flush out every poison deposited in my blood system as a result of evil food, in Jesus name.*
- *All that I have lost as a result of eating evil food, Father Lord let me have them back, in the name of Jesus.*
- *o God re-arrange any part of my body that has been fragmented by the power of infirmity, in Jesus' name.*
- *I curse to die, you the power of infirmity working in any part of my body, in the name of Jesus*
- *I speak destruction to the root of any infirmity planted by witchcraft powers in my life, in the name of Jesus.*

- *Every inherited sickness from my family lineage, dry to your roots, in the name of Jesus.*
- *Let the throne of Jesus Christ be established in every area of my life, in the name le, of Jesus.*

Day Four

Ps 107:20 He sent his word, and healed them, and delivered them from their destructions.

- *I break all curses of sickness and disease and command all inherited sickness to leave my body in the name of Jesus.*
- Every weapon of destruction fashioned against me, be destroyed by the fire of God, in the name of Jesus.
- I bind every spirit of death operating in my body in Jesus name

- *I resist every evil spirit of sickness and disease in my life and family in Jesus name*
- *I command every dead organ in my body to come alive in Jesus name.*
- *I command every evil monitoring gadget used against my health to be destroyed right now in Jesus name.*
- *I recover all the resources I have lost through sickness in Jesus name*
- *I release my body system from the cage of household wickedness in Jesus name.*
- *You evil stranger of sickness and disease in my body I command you to come out right now in the mighty name of Jesus.*
- *I cough and vomit out any evil and poisonous substance I have taken that is causing sickness and disease in my system in Jesus name*

- *Let every negative and evil material circulating in my bloodstream be evacuated in Jesus name*
- *I separate myself from every strange sickness and disease in Jesus name.*

Day Five

There shall no evil befall thee, neither shall any plague come nigh thy dwelling. Psalm 91:10

- *I separate myself from every genetic sickness in Jesus name*
- *Father I thank you for delivering me from sickness and disease in Jesus name.*
- *I refuse to be dominated by darkness in my health in Jesus name.*
- *I reign over sickness and disease, demons and death in Jesus name.*

- *Every wicked device against my health, receive fire right now and burn to ashes in Jesus name.*
- *My health, hear the word of the Lord; be restored back in Jesus name*
- *I stop the operations of enemy in my body by the power in the blood of Jesus Christ.*
- *I reject sickness and its manipulation in my life, in Jesus name.*
- *Any sickness or disease that wants to bring separation between me and God, I cast you out, in the name of Jesus*
- *You sickness, infirmity in my body, I command you to leave my life alone, in the name of Jesus.*
- *Power of God, uproot generation sickness from my life, in the name of Jesus. Arrows of sickness originating from idolatry, lose your hold, in the name of Jesus.*

- *Thou dark power of my father's house repeating sickness and affliction in my life, die, in the name of Jesus.*
- *Every cycle of sickness and affliction of the evil powers of my father's house, break, in the name of Jesus.*

Day Six

Jeremiah 17:14 Heal me, O LORD, and I shall be healed; save me, and I shall be saved: for thou art my praise. 1 Peter 2:24 Who his own self bare our sins in His own body on the tree, that we, being dead to sins, should live unto righteousness: by whose stripes ye were healed

Let any power on assignment to steal my health be exposed and be destroyed right now in Jesus name.

Powers that want to terminate my life through sickness or disease; I reject your mission in my life, go back to the sender, in the name of Jesus.

I nullify every prolonged sickness and infirmity in my body, in the name of Jesus

Any power on assignment to steal my health, receive frustration, in the name of Jesus.

I receive my healing by fire and by force; I am healed, in the name of Jesus.

I cast out every arrow of sickness flowing in my blood stream, in the name of Jesus.

I reject sickness and its manipulation in my life, in Jesus name.

Any power assigned to trouble my health, be destroyed, in the name of Jesus.

I denounce any sickness spoken into my life. I speak life unto myself, and I speak destruction unto all my enemies and all their weapons against me, in the name of Jesus.

Every owner of sickness in my life, carry it now in the name of Jesus.

I bind and paralyze every agent of infirmity in my life in the name of Jesus.

Every sickness transferred into my life in the dream, come out now and burn to ashes in Jesus' name.

Every arrow of infirmity against me go back to sender now in the name of Jesus.

Every power projecting diseases into my body fall down and perish in Jesus' name.

I command witchcraft affliction in my life, to catch fire and burn to ashes in Jesus' name.

Let every generational sickness that afflicts members of my family line, I cut you off by the power in the blood of Jesus.

Day Seven

Deuteronomy 7:1 5,"The Lord will keep you free from every disease. He will not inflict on you the horrible diseases you knew in Egypt."

Psalm 107:20 "He sent out His word and healed them, and delivered them from their destruction."

- *I command any sickness and diseases in my life destroying my finances to give up and die. in the name of Jesus.*
- *Any disease attached to my life at birth die now in Jesus name.*

- Stubborn spirits of infirmities following me about come out now, in Jesus name.
- Witchcraft Powers from my foundation cooking my flesh in any pot of darkness scatter now in Jesus name.
- Let the blood of Jesus Christ wash away any affliction that has gained access into my life because of my sins or that of my parents in Jesus name.
- Any sickness in my life programmed to send me to early grave, expire now, in Jesus name.
- Evil agenda to make sure I remain on this bed of affliction, enough is enough expire by fire, in Jesus name.
- Any bacteria or virus in my life, die now, in Jesus name.
- Any sickness inherited from my family background, out of my life, in Jesus name. I declare good health from the

crown of my head to the soul of my feet now, in Jesus name.

- Every evil personality, burning incense to afflict me with long term sickness somersault and die now, in Jesus name.
- Let every agenda of darkness over my life, scatter by thunder, in Jesus name. Any evil power that wants to renew negative covenant in my family, be destroyed right now, in Jesus name.
- Anything that has gone wrong in my life as a result of family evil pattern be corrected by fire, in Jesus name.
- Holy Ghost fire, separate me from family sickness and disease and attach me to healing, in Jesus name.
- Spirit of generational sickness from my family line operating in my life, be cancelled in Jesus name.

- *I refuse to allow any evil pattern programmed by any of my ancestor to trouble me, in Jesus name.*
- *I release my body from every curse of weekly, monthly and yearly sickness in my family, in Jesus name.*

After praying these prayers, be sure not to confess your doubt, fear or pain. At any point you feel the enemy trying to draw your attention to your pain, just go back to the scriptures and prayers in this book.

They overcame him by the blood of the lamb and by the word of their testimony Rev.12 11

ABOUT THE AUTHOR

John Ijeh is a dynamic preacher and teacher of God's word. He is the president of John Ijeh World Outreach. The Lord spoke to him on the 15th of December, 1997 to take His Word to the nations of the world and call God's people out of the world's captivity and satanic bondage. In response to this divine mandate, John ministers the word of God in churches, crusades, conferences and seminars and youth outreaches both within and outside Nigeria. He has also written several books. He lives in Lagos, Nigeria with his lovely wife, Mercy Ijeh and they are blessed with three children: Lovelyn, Praisel and Daniel.

About the Book

The word of God is life and healing to you. The Bible assures God's children of good health so that you don't have to be sick or live your life in pain and anguish.

As a child of God, you have all of God's authority to change your world with your words. And when you speak the Word of God by faith, it is just as if God is speaking.

Many people are battling against infirmities, sickness and diseases of which science have failed to provide a perfect solution. The word of God holds the solution to the health and wellbeing of humanity.

This book *"100 Healing Scriptures and Prayers for Self- Deliverance "* is a is the perfect resource to equip you with teaching and healing scriptures in order to receive your promised healing **and deliverance from every** oppressive force. It serves as a powerful weapon against sickness, diseases and infirmities.

It reveals to you;

- Relevant scriptures that guarantees your healing and deliverance
- Powerful warfare prayers for personal deliverance
- Powerful prayers to obtain divine healing for yourself and family
- How to exercise faith in difficult situations
- How to make the word of God work for you

Don't let the devil rob you of your good health, get a copy of this book and release God's divine healing, restoration and protection upon your life and family.

Printed in Great Britain
by Amazon